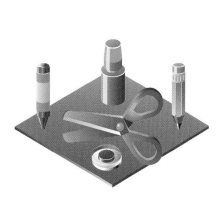

CHRISTMAS CRAFTS

by Jean Eick

Library of Congress Cataloging-in-Publication Data
Eick, Jean. 1947-
Christmas Crafts / by Jean Eick.
p. cm.
Includes index.
Summary: Provides instructions for making basic Christmas
crafts, such as pipe cleaner candy canes, bookmarks, and
napkin rings. Includes simple activities.
ISBN 1-56766-533-0 (alk. Paper)

1. Christmas decorations — Juvenile literature.
2. Handicraft — Juvenile literature.
[1. Christmas decorations. 2. Handicraft.]
I. Title.
TT900.C4E44 1998   98-15750
745.594'12 — dc21   CIP
                                                          AC

GRAPHIC DESIGN & ILLUSTRATION
Robert A. Honey, Seattle

PRODUCTION COORDINATION
James R. Rothaus / James R. Rothaus & Associates

ELECTRONIC PRE-PRESS PRODUCTION
Robert E. Bonaker / Graphic Design & Consulting company

CONTENTS

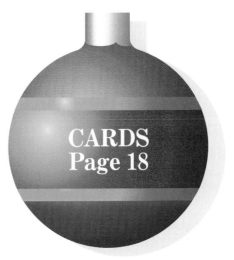

1 Christmas is a very special holiday for many people around the world. It's a time to be with family and friends. It's also a time for sharing and laughing. This book is full of great ideas you can make to celebrate this happy holiday. There are also ideas you can do with others.

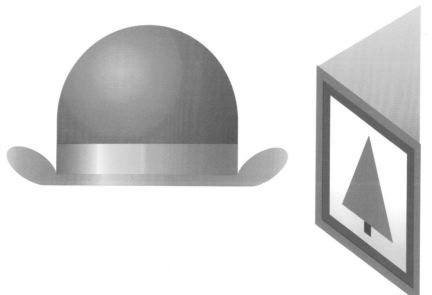

2 Before you start making any craft, be sure to read the directions. Make sure you look at the pictures too, they will help you understand what to do. Go through the list of things you'll need and get everything together. When you're ready, find a good place to work. Now you can begin making your crafts!

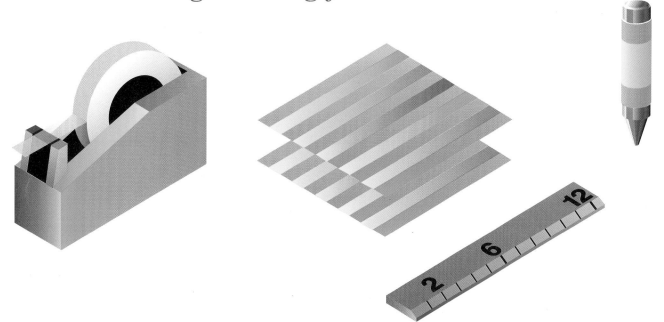

These decorations are easy to make. You can hang them on your Christmas tree or use them to decorate presents.

CANDY CANE

Things You'll Need

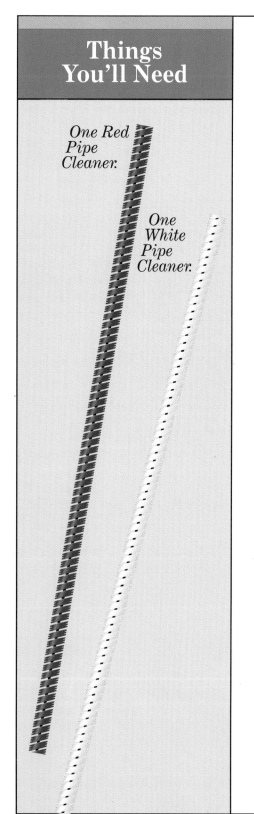

One Red Pipe Cleaner.

One White Pipe Cleaner.

1 Put the pipe cleaners side by side.

2 Then twist them together.

3

Do not twist
too tight,
just firm enough
to create a nice
and even spiral shape.

4

Bend the top
of the twisted
pipe cleaners.
Presto, a
candy cane!

Everyone knows the story of Rudolph's red nose. Now you can make fun Rudolph decorations.

RUDOLPH

Things You'll Need

Scissors.

2 Sheets of Brown Construction Paper.

A Shoe.

Glue.   Pencil.   Crayons or Markers.

1 On one sheet of construction paper draw around your shoe. This will be Rudolph's head.

2 On the other sheet draw around each hand. This will be Rudolph's antlers.

3 Cut out the shoe and hand prints.

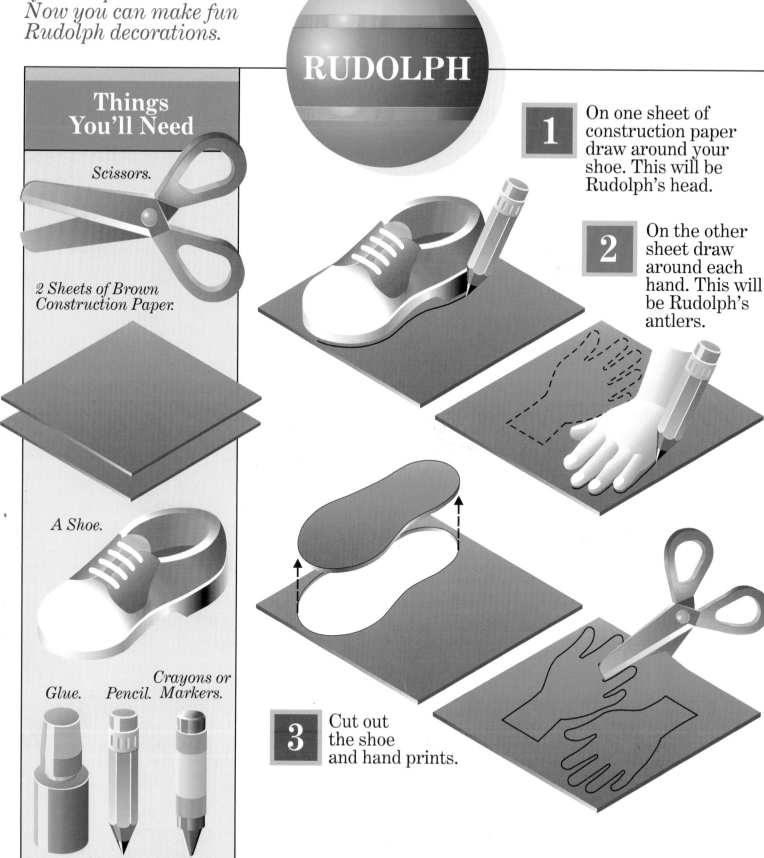

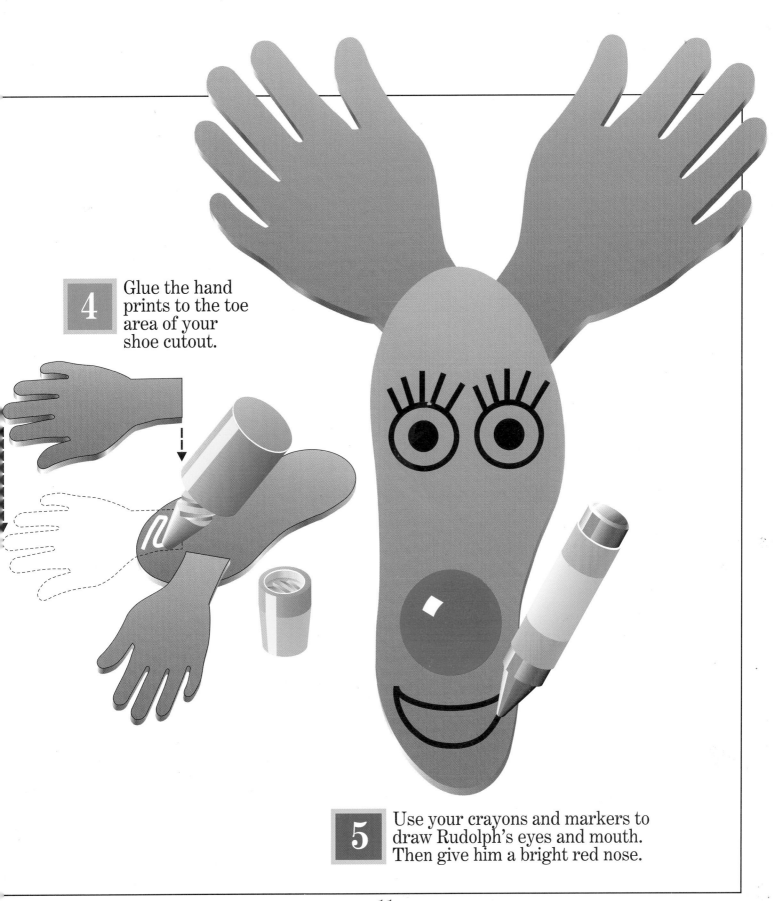

4 Glue the hand prints to the toe area of your shoe cutout.

5 Use your crayons and markers to draw Rudolph's eyes and mouth. Then give him a bright red nose.

You can hang these easy decorations almost anywhere — even on your tree!

CHRISTMAS STRINGS

Things You'll Need

Scissors.

3 Sheets of Construction Paper.
1 Red,
1 White,
1 Green.

Ruler.

Glue or Tape.   _Pencil._

1 With your ruler and pencil, divide each sheet of paper into 1 inch wide and six inch long strips.

2 Cut the sheets apart with your scissors.

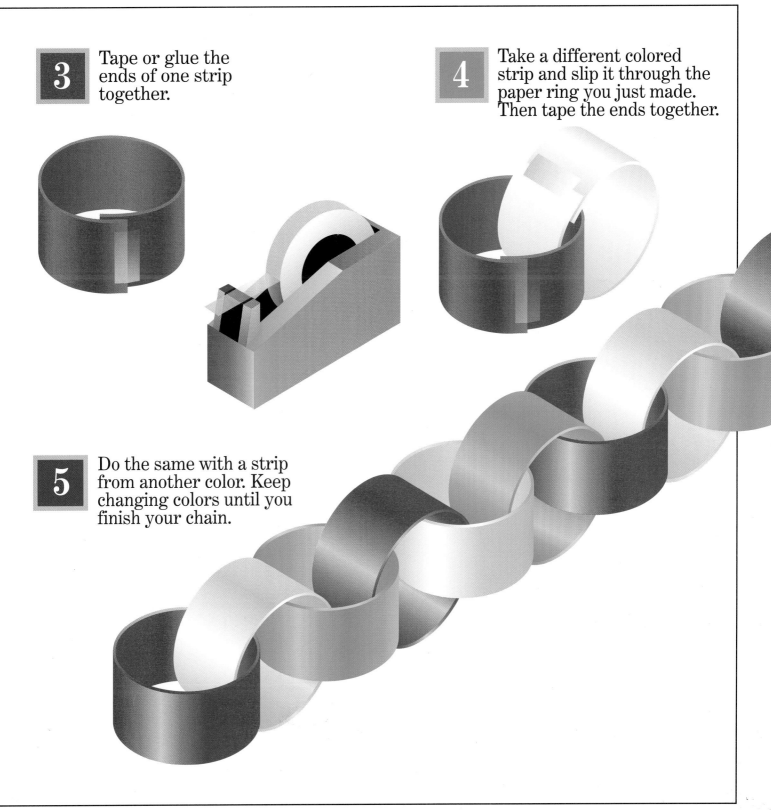

3 Tape or glue the ends of one strip together.

4 Take a different colored strip and slip it through the paper ring you just made. Then tape the ends together.

5 Do the same with a strip from another color. Keep changing colors until you finish your chain.

Try making these pretty gifts for your friends and teachers.

BOOKMARKS

Things You'll Need

Scissors.

Cereal Box.

Ribbon.

Ruler.

Hole Puncher.

Glue.

Pencil.

1 Cut out the front of cereal box.

BITES

Things for Decorating

Crayons or Markers.

Wrapping Paper.

Pictures and Stickers.

2 With your ruler and pencil, divide each sheet of paper into two inch wide and six inch long strips.

3 Cut the sheets apart with your scissors.

4 Decorate the strips however you want.

5 Use the hole puncher to make a hole in the top of the bookmark.

6 Tie a piece of ribbon through the hole.

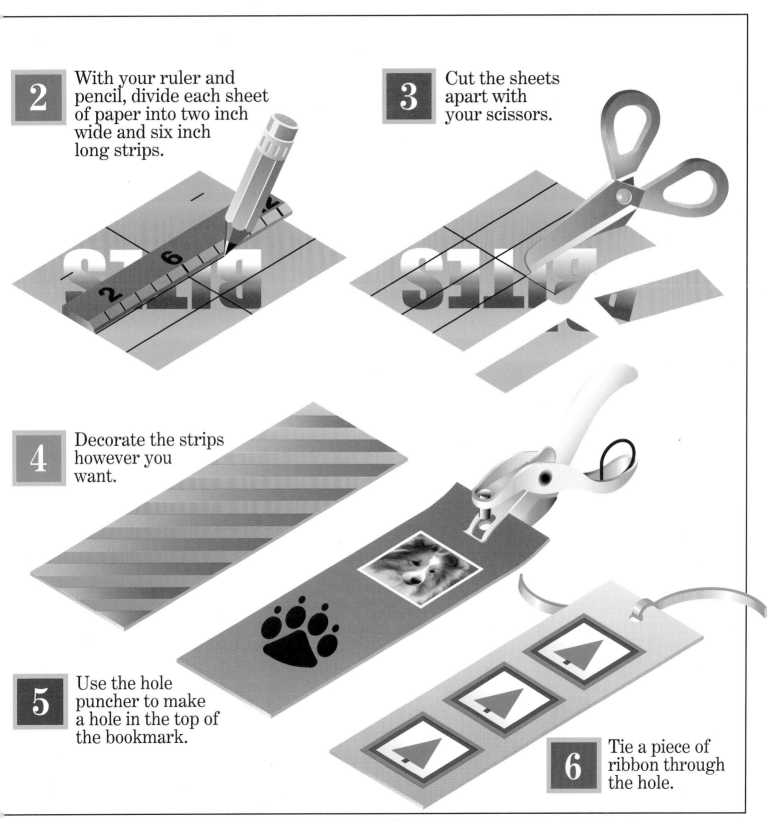

Napkin rings make special gifts for parents, grandparents, and teachers.

NAPKIN RINGS

Things You'll Need

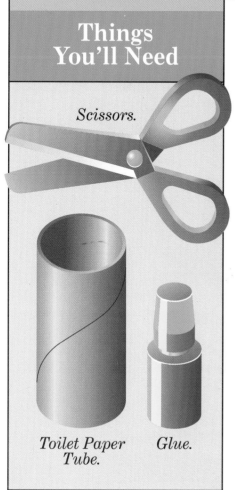

Scissors.

Toilet Paper Tube.

Glue.

1 Lay the tube flat. Use the scissors to cut the tube in half.

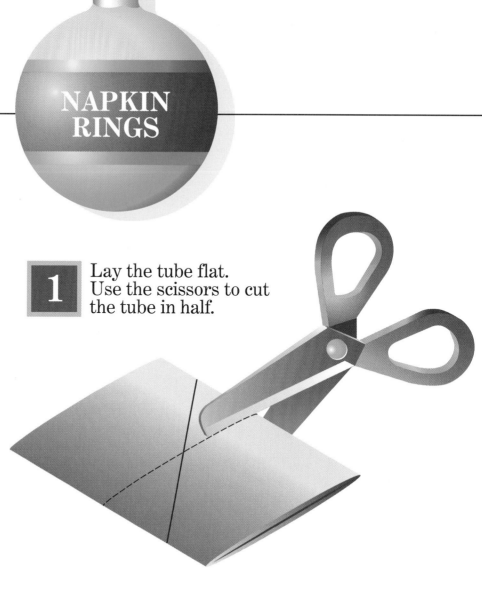

Things for Decorating

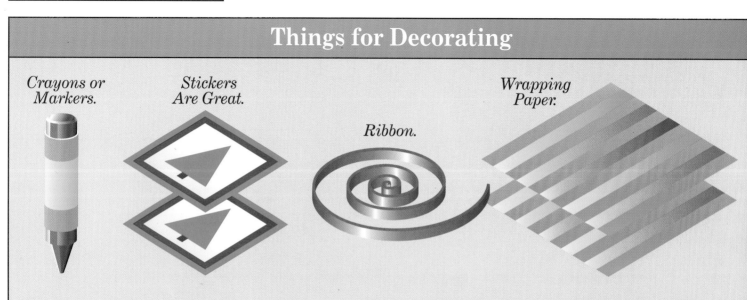

Crayons or Markers.

Stickers Are Great.

Ribbon.

Wrapping Paper.

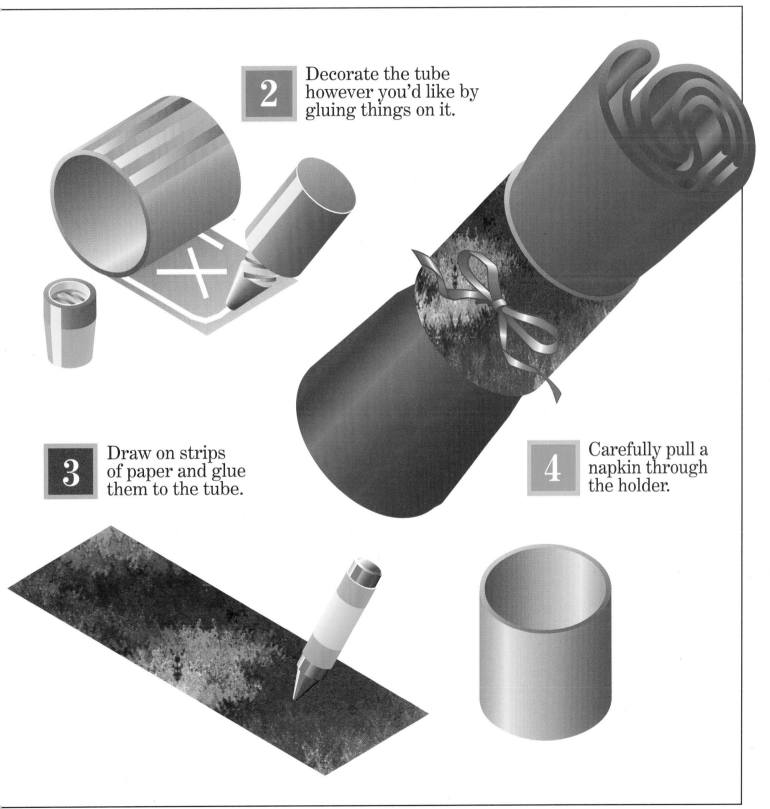

2 Decorate the tube however you'd like by gluing things on it.

3 Draw on strips of paper and glue them to the tube.

4 Carefully pull a napkin through the holder.

Giving cards is a very popular idea. You can send them to friends, teachers, and other special people.

CARDS

Things You'll Need

Scissors.

Crayons, Markers, or Paints. *Pencil.* *Glue.*

Construction Paper.

1 Fold the paper to the size you want your card to be. Folding it once will make a large card.

2 Folding it twice will make a small card.

3 Decorate the front of the card.

4 Write a message on the inside of the card. You can decorate the inside, too. Don't forget to sign your name.

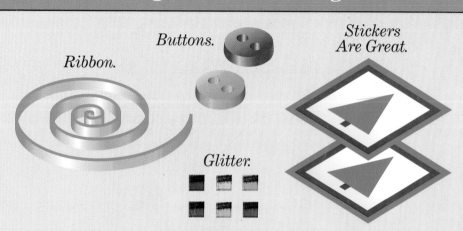

Things for Decorating

Ribbon.

Buttons.

Stickers Are Great.

Glitter.

Instead of making a square card, make one shaped like a Christmas tree!

1 Draw a jagged line from the bottom right corner to the top left corner.

2 Cut along the line with your scissors.

3 Now open the card. You should see a Christmas tree shape.

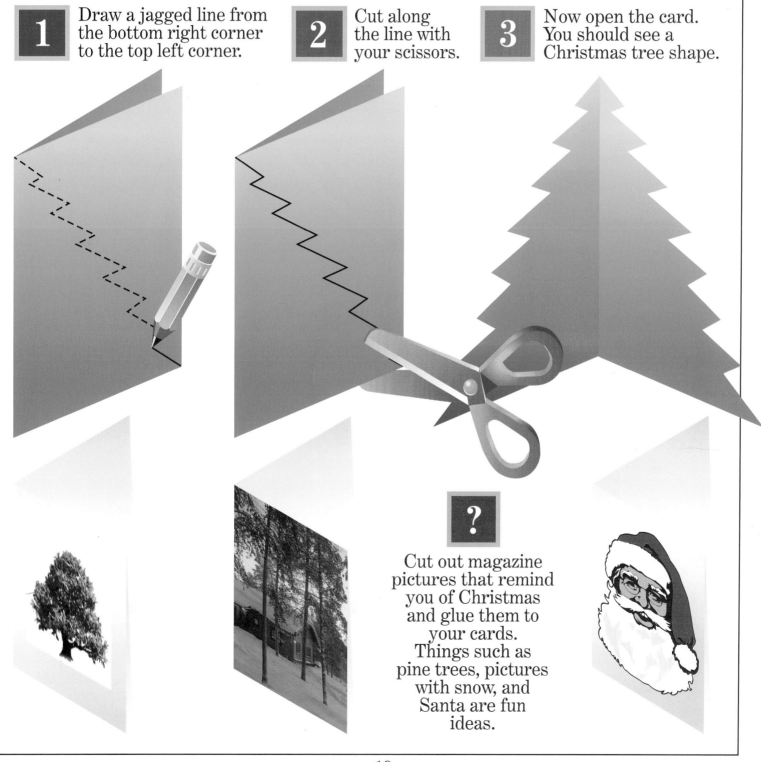

? Cut out magazine pictures that remind you of Christmas and glue them to your cards. Things such as pine trees, pictures with snow, and Santa are fun ideas.

You can even make your own envelopes to fit your cards!

ENVELOPES

Things You'll Need

Scissors.

Construction Paper, Wrapping Paper, or Paper Bag.

Pencil.

Tape or Glue.

Ruler.

To make a square envelope:

1 Cut out the front of a plain paper bag. It will take an 8 inch square piece of paper to hold a 5¼ inch square card.

2 Cut out a square 8 inches high and 8 inches across. Measure and put an "X" in the center of the square.

3 Fold three of the corners so they cover the "X". Tape or glue the corners so they'll stay in place.

4 Place your card inside, then fold the top down and tape it shut.

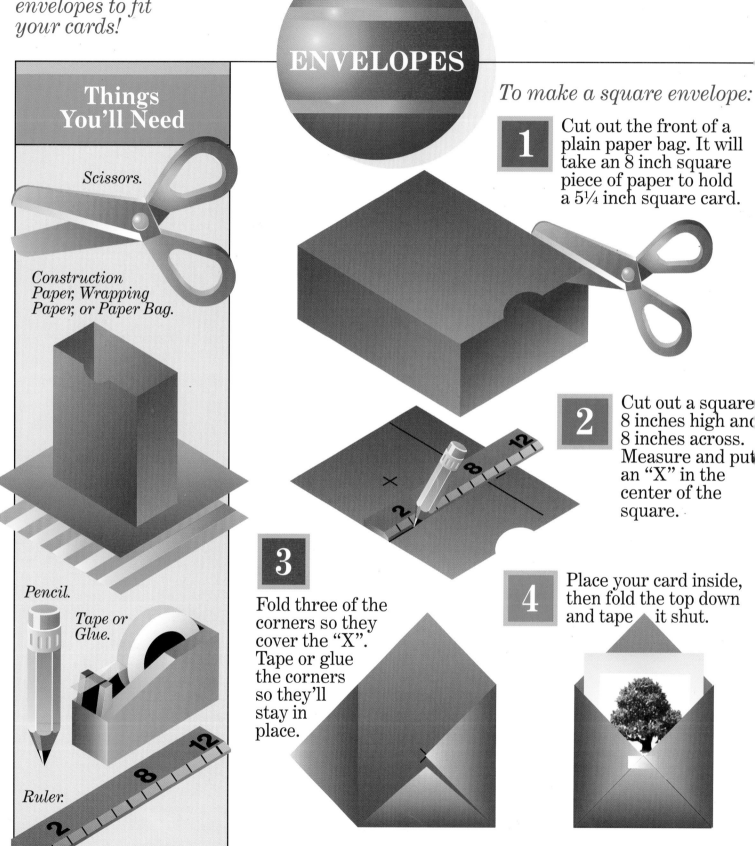

To make an envelope that isn't square:

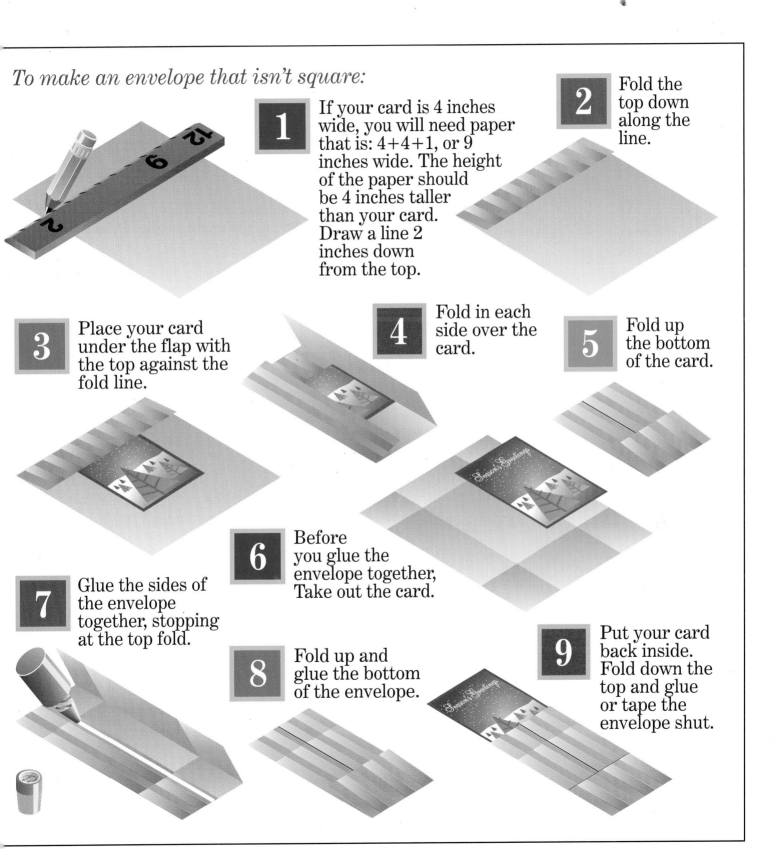

1 If your card is 4 inches wide, you will need paper that is: 4+4+1, or 9 inches wide. The height of the paper should be 4 inches taller than your card. Draw a line 2 inches down from the top.

2 Fold the top down along the line.

3 Place your card under the flap with the top against the fold line.

4 Fold in each side over the card.

5 Fold up the bottom of the card.

6 Before you glue the envelope together, Take out the card.

7 Glue the sides of the envelope together, stopping at the top fold.

8 Fold up and glue the bottom of the envelope.

9 Put your card back inside. Fold down the top and glue or tape the envelope shut.

ACTIVITIES

1 Have a card making party. Tell everyone to bring something different for decorating the cards. Then follow the directions on pages 18 and 19 to make lots of cards.

2 Decorate together. Have everyone choose a craft from this book. Then make the crafts while you listen to Christmas music. When everyone is finished, decorate the whole house or classroom.

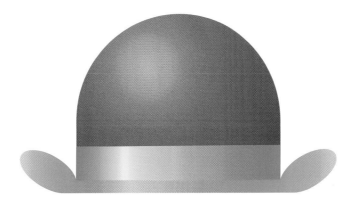

3 Play a dress-up game. Fill a bag full of things to wear. Make sure there are some silly hats and funny glasses! Have everyone sit in a circle, and play Christmas music. While the music is playing, pass the bag around. When the music stops, whoever is holding the bag must shut their eyes and take 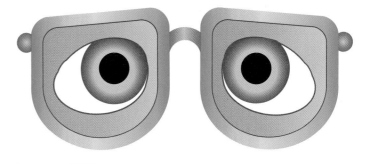 something out of the bag. They must wear it for the rest of the game. Keep playing until all the clothes are gone.